MUTSUO TAKAHASHI

SLEEPING SINNING FALLING

EDITED AND TRANSLATED BY

HIROAKI SATO

CITY LIGHTS BOOKS

SAN FRANCISCO

SLEEPING, SINNING, FALLING
Copyright © 1992 by Hiroaki Sato

First published by City Lights Books, 1992

Cover design by John Miller, Big Fish Books

Library of Congress Cataloging-in-Publication Data

Takahashi, Mutsuo, 1937-
    Sleeping sinning falling / by Mutsuo Takahashi ; translated
from the Japanese by Hiroaki Sato.
        p.   cm.
    Selected translation of the author's poetry.
    ISBN 0-87286-268-2 : $8.95
    1. Takahashi, Mutuso, 1937-   —Translations, English.
I. Satō, Hiroaki, 1942-   .   II.   Title.
PL862.A4212A27   1992
895.6'15—dc20   92-967
                                                  CIP

City Lights Books are available to bookstores through our
primary distributor: Subterranean Company. P. O. Box 160,
265 S. 5th St., Monroe, OR 97456. 503-847-5274. Toll-free orders
800-274-7826. FAX 503-847-6018. Our books are also available
through library jobbers and regional distributors. For personal
orders and catalogs, please write to City Lights Books,
261 Columbus Avenue, San Francisco, CA 94133.

CITY LIGHTS BOOKS are edited by Lawrence Ferlinghetti and
Nancy J. Peters and published at the City Lights Bookstore,
261 Columbus Avenue, San Francisco, CA 94133.

To Althea,
wherever you are

TABLE OF CONTENTS

PREFACE

by Hiroaki Sato

One slightly overcast afternoon in the spring of 1971 Rand Castile, now director of the Asian Art Museum of San Francisco, brought a Japanese poet to my apartment, which was then on 78th Street, in Manhattan. All I remember from that first encounter with the poet, Mutsuo Taskahashi, is his mellifluous voice as he read "Dream of Barcelona: My Ancient World." So memorable was his voice nonetheless that of all the Japanese poets I have translated, he has become the one I have translated the most: *Poems of a Penisist* (Chicago Review Press, 1975), *A Bunch of Keys* (The Crossing Press, 1984), and now this, the third selection.

Mellifluous voice alone does not, of course, make a poet compelling. I soon found that Takahashi has, among other things, a high sense of drama — the sense that a poem is not something intended for the poet's satisfaction of his inner self alone but for others' partaking as well. In this Takahashi stands out from many poets writing in Japan today, much of whose work remains "heavy with Parnassian and Symbolist echoes," as Geoffrey O'Brien has noted, or else self-servingly opaque with a deliberate barrenness copied from "The Waste Land" or with Surrealist obscurantism. It is no accident that Takahashi has had a longstanding interest in Greek drama, nō, and kyōgen. Euripides' *Medea* in the translation he revised for the stage has been produced in Athens, Rome, London, and New York. His most recent book, published in 1991, consists of three dramas: an adaptation of Yeats' play, *At the Hawk's Well*, a kyōgen, and a nō inspired by Georges Bataille's *Le Procès de Gil de Rais* and Carl Dreyer's film, *La Passion de Jeanne d'Arc*.

In late 1985 when the Committee for International Poetry sponsored "A Festival of Japanese Poetry" in New York, Takahashi was one of the six participants. On that occasion I asked him what he thought of the Japanese language, poetry and translation, and what his latest trip to the United States meant to him. Here are some of the things he said.

"At the PEN American Center reception I said Japanese is an 'isolated language,' but later I regretted that I hadn't explained this well. Much of Japanese vocabulary comes from the South Pacific islands, and its syntax is close to those of Ural-Altaic languages, such as Korean. But where Japanese ultimately belongs is subject to a great variety of opinions. When I said Japanese is a language 'suspicious as to its behavior,' I meant that a Japanese poet is forced to accept the state of belonging in no definite place. If we could have a sense of belonging, we'd be relieved, but for the moment we can't be conclusive about its primary origin. So I should have said that as a Japanese poet I don't know where to 'position' the Japanese language. I didn't at all mean to imply that I am proud that Japanese is an 'isolated language.'

"Generally, it is said that translation of poetry is impossible, and poets believe this to a considerable degree. As it happens, I don't consider poetry and translation in exaggerated terms. A language is a 'borrowed thing,' a medium. I make a distinction between poesy and poem; poesy is something that comes from over there, and when it does, you become a receptacle, at the same time making your mother tongue a receptacle, and return that 'something' in the form of a poem. Poesy itself doesn't have a form. A poet gives it a form. To what degree he can express the poesy he received through a poem he writes can't be known, but the poem gives something to the translator and turns into another language. In this sense, the act of writing a poem itself is a form of translation.

"So to a great extent I am positive about having my poems translated. A translation gives my poem another refraction, and I sometimes make an unexpected discovery in it.

"I have been to this country a few times before, but they were trips mainly for me to *receive* what I saw and heard — receive various things from America. This time, however, it was a trip in which I offered myself, through my poems, and had American reactions to it. I don't know what kind of effect I've had on people here, but on this trip my relation to this country ceased to be one-sided, and I feel some connection to it has been made."

Takahashi has received four literary prizes: Rekitei Prize for the book of poems Ōkoku no Kōzō (The Structure of the Kingdom), in 1982; Yamamoto Kenkichi Prize for the stage script Princess Medea, in 1987; Yomiuri Literary Prize for the collection of haiku and tanka Keiko Onjiki (Practice/Drinking Eating), in 1988; and Takami Jun Prize for the book of poems Usagi no Niwa (The Garden of Rabbits), in 1988.

Some of the poems translated here have appeared first in Bomb (summer 1986), Tyuonyi (2 & 4), Paul Bowles, and in the inaugural issue of City Lights Review. Those interested in my essay on translating Takahashi may turn to "Imagery: A Translator's Quandary," in the March 1986 issue of Japan Society Newsletter.

I am grateful to Mutsuo Takahashi for answering questions on his poems, Bob Sharrard for inviting me to submit a manuscript, and Robert Fagan for improving my translations.

New York
1992

SLEEPING, SINNING, FALLING

"Why are you angry, and why has your
countenance fallen? If you do well, will you not
be accepted? And if you do not do well, sin is
crouching at the door . . . ." *Genesis 4:6-7*

I

From the slightly everted skin of the sleeper's eyelid
noisy deaths, dark deaths, muddy deaths
all screaming, wrangling, climb up toward you

The sleeper, in a rocking chair,
whacked by a club of sunlight,
his nape blood-congested with innumerable spots,
his whole body a golden numbness, sleeps.

Fingers curled leisurely inward,
toes arched, eyelids dreamily closed —
from these eversions of nails and skin
peers a red red laziness.

The sleeper's white marrow
is being eaten by cruel swarming ants.
At times the tongue of the sun grown gentle
licks his pores.

The sleeper, in the fervid darkness,
like a full ripe pomegranate, giving a glimpse of himself, sleeps.
Dropping like a sweep from the high skylight that's pushed up
the light cut out in skylight shape
captures half of his sweaty face.
Sleep — concentrating on that act,
his flushed face looks almost pained.
Adorned with spouting beads of sweat
the golden downy hair in a tight mass glistens.
As he repeats his regular breathing
his eyelids, lips, nostrils, nail gaps —
from every everted part dark heavy deaths sometimes show.
Filling the labyrinth of red blood throughout his body
with noisy deaths, this man
grits his white teeth.
He opens his mouth, and at once his tongue
teems with cruel ants.
It's as if he's saying:
Sleeping is a struggle, a ceaseless
terrifying struggle, with eternal death.

The sun collides with the space around the door left open,
causing blood congestion, hesitating.
In the moist hay in the livestock barn,
which emits a golden smell, still not dry,
sleeper, what is it that you emanate?
The coarse shirt soiled from harsh labor
in the sun's forenoon, and your exposed chest
so sweaty, looking almost pained —
from the reddish darkness of your half-open lips
escapes something with an animal smell — is that death,
     ceaseless death?
In your red sleep, what kind of unknown stairs
at earth's bottom does your heightened lust
go down, or go up?
Your tightly gripped, knobby fingers —

who will those thick fingers kill, dirt collected under their nails?
What invisible knife, of what weight, are they gripping?
The earth that embraces you in your terrifying sleep,
the earth like everted folds of flesh — what is it?
What does plowing mean? What is sowing?
A brother who shares the same blood with you? Cousins who
        fight among themselves for blood?
A woman impregnated with your glistening semen?
Sleeper, in the livestock barn, in the disintegrating darkness,
in the pent-up smell, in the immobile, young afternoon,
this side of your face that is visible, flushed,
you who are moaning like mud,
are you yourself the dark death in you,
or are you life?

In the sleeper sleep ripens
just as in a leather bag cheese ripens —
he's in the pouring sun,
his heavy body rocking in a rattan chair.

From his everted eyelids, from his half-open mouth
sleep peers out, flame-colored like a cut wound.
Around it sleep's ripe odor almost suffocates.

The pomegranates have withered, the olives have fallen asleep,
the souls of the elderberries have also gone to sleep, deep in
the earth.
Adding soulless chips from withered, withered trees,
listening to the tragic sound of souls popping,
in the rocking chair, undulating, he sleeps.
Asleep, blood engorged right below his thin skin,
he continues to fall in a red dark pitfall.
Behind him, the large glass-door reflects the fire,
and in the dark garden the lusts of the plants
snap, snap, as they continue to wither.

The sleeper is a solid oven made of bricks.
What's licking the wall, the flesh, from within, flickering,
is blood's, agate's, death's, whispering flame's tongue
— From the blindfolded peep-hole, that is visible —

Held in the gentle folds of burning flames
and slowly ripening, the dream yeast —
outside this oven emitting the fragrant smell
is a howling darkness.

From the sleeper's arched eyelashes
dangle
sticky sugar-cakes of sleep.

The ants of death fight for their places on them,
hanging from the icicles of sleep,
numbed by the sweet sleep.

The sleeper, in the fire-red pitfall,
is fighting these invisible, tiny enemies.
His fingers, as if annoyed, rub his eyelids.

Heaven's overflowing tides! Tides!
Distant from the freshly born, aquamarine sky,
curling up like a fetus,
how far in this bloody dark pitfall will this sleeper
continue to fall?

This man, who continues to fall,
continues to fall through layers of sleeping cities,
through the sea where broken ships are entangled in seaweed,
through dreams entangled in the strands of hair
of the mummies who continue to sleep for thousands of years.

II

You're running away, big brother.
No matter how far you get away,
you are running
here, on my face.

Ah, poor big brother.
Where are you now?
I can almost see you —
you, trying to get away from the earth that turned pale,
ears covered with hands, eyes full of blood,
blindly rushing away.
I'd like to come and kiss you.
But I'm no more.
Because, from behind me, you suddenly swung down a piece of
     heavy iron
my face scattered away in various directions.
Through the wide night I look for you
but because I have become too many
I can no longer find you anywhere.

Big brother,
you put me in a swing
and thrust me off into the sky as best you could.
Why did you do such a frightening thing?
When father asked, you didn't answer.
When he said he heard a voice of blood, you covered your ears.
Big brother,
wasn't that your voice?
The spiral stairs continuing into earth's deep deep bottom —
it's you who are rushing down them.
I understand you.
My faces, there are many of them.
But I have no voice.
Besides, my faces go on increasing without number.

You can't sleep,
big brother, but you aren't the only one.
Since you swung iron down on my head
my eyes have remained open.
I am always awake.
Through night's forest, under dark foliage,
over the face of secretive water,
to the end of lonesome fields where a ravaged moon shines,
my eyes follow, however far it may be.
What my open eyes are looking for is you,
your heart as lonely as a wolf.

Midnight, awake under foliage
and quietly weeping — that's me.
Why hadn't I told you this?
That I love you so much.
But you always looked forbidding,
plowing the earth, your back turned to me.
I didn't have a chance to say it.
Ah, if I'd known you were suffering so,
if I'd had a little more courage!
Big brother, where in the world is Nod?
Even if you go there, you won't be able to clean
your hands of my blood.
Your ears will not forget my scream.
Even if you suffer,
that isn't my wish.
Big brother, I'd like to say to you:
Ah, how much I love you!

Big brother,
you never once smiled for me.
You never faced me and wept.
If you'd done that,
I'd have jumped into your arms,
and holding each other we'd have wept.
Then, hand in hand,
we'd have gone to the end of the earth.
We are awake,
but the two of us are forever alone.

I put my hands to my mouth,
shout at the top of my voice.
But you blindly run away.
My voice becomes hoarse,
but you don't listen.

You cover your ears,
but what you are hearing
is not my voice.
The direction in which you are escaping
is red with the sin you committed.

Forest,
trees,
gentle arms, legs, swarms of rustling nerves,
world's most sensitive souls,
you must know
how much I loved him.
When the two of us passed through you,
you touched my arms, his shoulders,
and shook your leaves, your branches.

How carefully
I removed those leaves, those branches
from his shoulders, from his neck —
when in your depths, under wild strawberry leaves
he put his mouth to the spout of an overflowing spring
and made his throat guggle
how gently I looked down at his nape
trembling as his throat guggled —
when he felt sated after lunch and dozed
and a viper crawled up to his bare feet,
how violently I killed it —
many days, many nights
of ours, his and mine. . . .
forest, you must know

The dead one's hardening legs on my shoulders,
his teeth champing, bloodless lips opening, closing, below me,
I continue to go down, the stairs cold on the soles of my feet —
does this undulating spiral
continue to the bottom of the earth, to the deep bottom
of the nauseatingly heavy fog of — what darkness?
I now can't even utter a voice.
My ears have the lids of a silence
as frightening as the clamor of the city of sin.
A stifling   no, rather
desolate   heart-crushing anxiety.
Suddenly I put him down,
fall on my knees, hug him, kiss him:
with my wet hot mouth I open his cold mouth,
with my hot teeth strike his cold teeth,
with my burning tongue seek his frozen tongue of death.
The moving flesh of a tongue entwines the numbing gaff of
          the other,
the frothing hot saliva sucks up the viscous liquid of death.
And now, do these descending stairs truly descend
or do they ascend?
Now, is the one alive holding the one dead,
is the live mouth being sucked by the dead mouth?
Out of the terrifying sky
spills overabundant light —
your eyes no longer swallow it.
Absorbing bundles of gentle light to the full
your eyes, dark, brown, used to move vivaciously.
Now, everted upward from death's rigidity,
what are they seeing
within the pale eyelids, in the draped secret chambers of
          red blood?
A forest of intricate optical nerves,
clusters of branches of heavy blood,
foliages of brain cells collapsed and frothing,
the storm of your rustling brain — in the midst of it all

a running shadow that's getting away,
that's me, that's me, that's me, that's me.
Looking down, sunk in thought,
at your face on moist dead leaves with viscid red blood
      congealed on it —
that's me.
Your legs on shoulder, continuing the heavy walk — that's me.
Eyes blood-shot, ears covered with hands — that's me.
Washing the hands in a stream where the moon glitters —
      that's me.
Pushing open your dead lips with lips,
pushing your teeth with teeth, groping for your tongue with
      tongue — that's me.
Putting tooth-marks on your thighs — that's me.
Hugging you violently — that's me.
To these me's you are calling from beyond the dark storm
in a voice that doesn't form a voice.
Where in the world are you?
Where am I?

The you of mine alone,
the you that I made, that is, the you that is death —
tracing that you with the bellies of my fingers, I sprinkle
    the earth.
I put your ankles side by side, join your hands on your chest,
and scatter the earth up to your gentle Adam's apple.
Filling with earth, squish-squish,
the space around your soft hair collecting light,
I leave out only the vacant, open, tiny mouth and the eyes.
Kid brother, over your heavy sleep, someday a hazel will grow,
gorses will luxuriate, achyranthes will run rampant.
Just as you, turning into thickets, birds' nests, and pools
    of water,
will not be forgotten from the sky here,
I will continue to wander, ever under the weight
of this ground that is you yourself.

Father said, Go to Nod,
murderer of your kid brother, you go to Nod,
you have no other place than Nod to go to.
But where's Nod?
What in the world do you mean by Nod?
Don't know, no one knows.
But since I've murdered my kid brother
I have no other place to go than Nod.
Ah, Nod, Nod, my Nod is parched.
For no reason my Nod is parched, dammit.
Nod's parched, where in the world do you mean by Nod?
That parched Nod, that parchedness is Nod.
The always parched Nod, that's Nod.
Because you are a murderer of your kid brother,
go to parched Nod, to the parchedness of Nod,
to Nod of fire.
But, Nod,
what in the world do you mean by Nod?

Murdered kid brother,
your face fills as much of the earth as is known.
At the end of the wandering of long years and months,
I finally reach
the scar on your forehead, the spring of blood bubbling up,
      spilling over.
My painful escape was to hide in your wound.
My dirty hands are for the first time cleansed
when immersed deep in your blood.
The peace of you and me
rests in our sin.

A white, delicate throat
was twitching — that I remember.

Not to let my receding fury come to an end,
with one blow of iron, I made him eternally unable to talk.
Then, my hands dirtied by the blood
blindly stacked branches and nettles upon him.

                                                    But

                      did I do anything?
Was he murdered for sure?
At that time, in the terrifying turn of blood
I understood nothing,
but someone's large hands came along
and carried him away in that instant
between my decision and the blow, I think.
When night comes, beyond the thickets of leaves of the forest,
in the dark that floats over the horizon, his wide-open eyes
tremble as if they want to say something, I think.
Despite myself I rise tiptoe
and feel myself filled with a fragment of voice like frothy blood
        stuck in the throat.
But, now someone stands
between him and me.

III

Deep in the eyes of the man staring at the fire,
burning, time falls,
and in the heart-shaped funnel
blood, like a weight, continues to fall.

Sorrel vines fall,
acorns fall,
fragments of snow, from sky's cracks, fall,
moaning, winds, through the dark, fall,

fall on a stand of cypresses,
on gleaming railway tracks,
on a field of turnip leaves,
on a frothing, rough sea.

Wandering birds fall,
Sabine's gulls, snipes, leaf-like sky travelers fall.
Did you not see the sky-blue bird the size of a thumb
that comes falling on your palm?

Falling away —
The one loved buries his face on the lover's chest.
Listen, what's that?
The lover gently toys with the hair of the one loved.
Well, that's a soul falling away from darkness to darkness.

Loves fall,
holding each other, lovers fall,
love's sweet nothings fall,
passions, shouting, fall.

Ah, someone, catch them please.
They fall, endlessly fall,
from darkness to darkness, from abyss to abyss,
fall, like pebbles, like embers fall.

Darkness falls to darkness, valley to valley,
sky's crack to sky's crack,
they fall, from abyss to abyss,
to lightlessness, to the souls' dark night,
snow, without a sound, falls,
winds, shouting, fall,
stars fall, birds fall,
angels, bird-shaped, fall,
loves, holding each other, headlong,
holding their breath, fall.

Crime is to fall,
like a streak of light, like a scar made with glass,
glistening with a sharp pain, it's to fall without limit;
it's to fall, holding each other,
loving, blindly, to the darkness, to the depths,
to a curse, to hatred, to a community of loathing,
it's to fall.

The tears of love are heavy.
Innocent love may be pulled up, on rainbow-hued wings,
to joy, to above the daybreak clouds,
but the love fulfilled by avoiding God's countenance,
sensually groaning, ecstatically arching back,
falls through dark timelessness.

The depths are an annihilation.
What gleams there are putrefying flesh
and the maggots that crawl up on it and wriggle.
Our love that falls — why is it not as light as heat haze,
as heavenly as Iris?

Loves are torn apart.
Holding each other, the two
are endlessly torn apart.
Angels of love, their wings wrenched off, fall.

Shouts fall through the sky.
Night, loves fall,
love's sweet nothings, swear-till-all's-blue's,
promised things fall.

Lovers fall,
the big clock under which lovers have trysts
falls like fragments of snow,
birds of glass, hitting hard soil, shatter.

Hazelnuts fall,
acorns fall,
the snow falls on the face of the muttering dark sea,
birds of the sky fall away,
a star falls away like a torch through the void.

Please look at us.
We are falling away.
Not to your palm of loving-kindness
but to the center of our weight are we falling away.
Please keep looking at us.

The sky is open.
From some unseen place the snow falls toward us.
In the terrifying void it gleams for a while
and a moment afterward, no one knows.

Even those stars that fall away, burning,
are they any different from fragments of snow?
Angels fall; devils, attracted by the centroid
of their own beauty, arms on their chests, fall.

Falling away,
we keep falling away,
becoming an inverse cone, slenderer toward the bottom,
falling away toward the depths like a flower adrift,
like a spear, by its own weight
shining, we fall.

from
A BUNCH OF KEYS

WINTER EROS

If it is true that he was born
of a mother named Decline,
the black of winter is appropriate as his color.
His breath is the searing wind of the dark night,
and his voice, the hailstones that strike and pain the cheeks.
The flappings of the wings on his back, the twang of his
        bow-string —
all such things are unrecorded events in the darkness.
But that, just as black paint contains red,
the dark invariably has a spot of fire which continues to burn
throughout the night, will be proved in the morning
when sparkling ash is found laid over the earth,
silvery as the hair of his father Fertility.

THREE CURSES FOR THOSE TO BE BORN

"Be Afraid of Fish"
Be afraid of fish.
Be afraid of fish that have no voice.
Be afraid of fish that are soul-shaped.
Be afraid of fish that are the alphabet at the bottom of
    man's memory.
Be afraid of fish that are more aged than man or tortoise.
Be afraid of fish that came into being when water did.
Be afraid of fish that know every strand of bog moss, yet keep
    silent about it.
Be afraid of fish that are more shadowy than the shadow in the
    water which is more dreamy than the dream.
Be afraid of fish that silently slip in and out of your
    nightly dream.
Be afraid of fish that remain in the water even when they mate.
Be afraid of fish whose gills continue to move even while asleep.
Be afraid of fish that move their mouths, afloat, with their air
    bladders, in watery heaven.
Be afraid of fish that are softer than lovers when caught.
Be afraid of fish, the foul feeders, that swallowed a god's
    phallus that was twisted off and discarded.
Be afraid of fish that shed human tears when broiled on fire.
Be afraid of fish that are your fathers, that are your mothers.
Be afraid of fish that occupy your entirety the morning after you
    were bored by fish.
Be afraid of fish that remain fish-shaped even after turning
    into bones.
As for the fish bones, put them on your palms and return them
    to the water,
going down, barefoot, to the beach where your sewage pipe
    empties itself.

"Wheat King"
I am the Wheat King.
My dried-up small face is half rotten in the darkness of earth.
Extending, transparent and arched, from the black, cold
      putrefaction, are the buds of disease.
Feeling the air of early spring, the buds grow sparsely and turn
      pale as a dead man's brow.
When the wind becomes warm, the feeble wheat seedlings catch
      fever at once.
The ears of wheat, broiled with high fever and emaciated, are
      pulled off by women's violent thigh-like fingers,
and are slashed, slashed with flails all day long.
Stone mortars smash me, and when I become wheat flour of
      poor coloration, I'm put through sieves.
I am kneaded with water, baked in ovens, and, as shabby
      noodles, carried into mouths with rotten teeth.
The left-overs are thrown, with saliva, into vats, and are made to
      ferment grumblingly.
I become a coarse liquor, go down men's sinuous throats, and
      wander with their muddy blood.
I am disfigured life that is poured out from man into woman at
      the end of travels of sufferings.
I am great death that fills that disfigured life.
Take me from this seed pot.

      "Those with Wings"
Those with wings
those with long beaks
those that fly across clamorously moving their beaks up
      and down
those with pointed eyes
those that come and go between the city of life and the
      city of death
those that cross over both into purity and into filth
those that circle man's sky cautiously
those that, with scaly legs, alight on the sandy beach of time

those that clutch pebbles with crooked nails
those that stand about in flocks
those that ruffle up their feathers, vying for food laid out by
    the gods
those that are treacherous and easily surprised
those that flap up all at once
those that are bathed in overflowing scarlet as they dive into
    the sunset
those that chase the shooting stars
those that reach the shore of the spirits throughout the night
those that fly up, holding white-haired, wrinkled babies in
    their beaks
those that fly down, like frost, to the ridges of roofs in dawn
those that push orphan souls into the crotches of women
    sloppily asleep:
shoot those suspicious shadows

WE ARE DEAD

We are dead.
With a worm-eaten pomegranate and a dried-up beetle
    beside me,
my brain, in a glass jar with a lid,
and my memories, in the clamor of a plaza,
gradually clear.

Plaza:
an obscene gathering for onions and edible thistles,
for decrees and gossip, for weddings and executions.
Both the houses and the people had to live, close to one another,
whether for loving or for tormenting.

Now, far from the plaza,
but in a location where its bustle can be heard a little,
we are seated, still close to one another,
protected by night's companions:
owls and snakes of the earth.

What were we in the past?
The only recourse with which to tell us apart,
those sweet parts of us, are rotten,
only the remaining holes
open to the gods' empty heaven.

Our sweet parts were
always moist, gleaming.
Rubbing each other fiercely, sobbing,
twitching, they poured out voluminous blood.
Memories always smell of blood.

Are those that went out of the holes memories,

or are the memories us?
We have all failed to become gods. As such,
we are ejected in wooden boats into the river
which becomes a waterfall and falls off the end of the ocean.

If that's the case, who's this one here?
Wearing the hat of a traveler of the underground country,
holding a spindle and a stone axe, his arms crossed,
and lying like this,
is he no more than a skinbag after my evaporation?

We are no longer what we were,
our bed now a boat, as water passes,
the water hugging sickly snails,
a seemingly peaceful landscape where a snipe with long shins
        stands forever,
and a feverish sandstorm every spring.

The one who once reigned over us passes,
and his giant head and genitals in bas-relief are scraped off.
What's eternal is the reaching-up of the flames burning
        cow dung.
Happy are those
who surround that fire in a reed house.

But here the fire is out.
What's here is soil and water
and the cold heavy smell of putrefaction.
The bunch of keys to the secret of the kingdom
lies in that chest-tightening evil smell.

The secret is that this place called life
is in due time to become the realm of death,
that white bones washed by time will cover the earth,
under the heavenly dome where a plethora of eyelashes
of fossilized stars flutter.

But those who surround the fire on the earthen floor
should concentrate on adding fodder to the fire.
What supports the incessant revival and the brilliance
of the flames that radiate their expressions
is our silence.

PYTHAGORAS BEANS

1

"Don't eat beans,"
our teacher said,
"because the beans belong to the dead."

"Don't eat the dead,"
our teacher did not say,
"because the dead belong to the beans."

"Eat the dead,"
our teacher did not say, either,
"because the dead do not belong to the beans."

"Eat beans,"
our teacher of course did not say,
"because the beans do not belong to the dead."

"Eat your teacher,"
the dead did not say,
"because your teacher does not belong to the beans."

"Don't eat your teacher,"
the beans did not say, either,
"because your teacher belongs to the dead."

2

Our memory of our teacher is linked from the beginning to the
beans. Our teacher appeared on this island just when the beans
were being harvested. Standing at the bean-flailing place located
almost at the center of this generally bean-shaped island, he
shouted "like a popping bean under the clear sky" (that is,

"suddenly"). Silly pods of beans, stop eating beans! The residents whose mouths were stuffed with beans, as it was lunchtime just then, were surprised, their eyes becoming as round "as beans that have absorbed as much salt water as they can." It was because on this island where, as its name, the Island of Beans, suggests, nothing but beans could be harvested, people got by mainly with beans both as their staple and secondary food, to stop eating beans was tantamount to stopping living. Our teacher continued to pop out his words like a pop-gun at the residents who stopped masticating their beans, taken aback as they were like birds shot at by pop-guns. Don't you know that beans are the food of the dead and the dogs! Give what belongs to the dead and the dogs to the dead and the dogs! Man doth not live by beans only! When they heard this much, the residents tried to beat our teacher, each with a bean-flail. But there were then several people who were touched by the words of our teacher, who immediately spat out the beans mixed with saliva from their mouths and surrounded our teacher to protect him from the bean-flails. This island, which had been peaceful ever since the beans and the bean pods were created, split into the Bean Group and the Anti-Bean Group and plunged into an age to be called by later generations the Civil War of Beans. The members of the Anti-Bean Group built a hall by weaving together the bean stalks in the waste land not taken up by bean patches and started a clean life neither planting nor eating beans. Chewing tree roots and sipping dew on the grass, our teacher shouted. Beans were clean, and men were clean. But you devoured the beans and sullied them, and sullied yourselves. Therefore, you must repent, and by respecting beans and staying away from them, you must cleanse the beans, cleanse yourselves! Chewing tree roots and sipping dew on the grass, the believers recited. Beans were clean, and men were clean. But we devoured the beans and sullied them, and sullied ourselves. Therefore, we must repent, and by respecting beans and staying away from them, we must cleanse the beans, cleanse ourselves! This great chorus rang throughout the island mornings and evenings, and as the Anti-Bean Group continued to increase mornings and evenings, the bean patches visibly went wild. The words of wisdom on the beans our teacher gave us on every and each occasion cannot all be recorded here. Ten years later, by counting them by the number of beans, when only a single bean patch was left on the island, our teacher abruptly declared: It is no longer appropriate to call us the Anti-Bean group. In fact, we are the true Bean-Group. The reason for this is that by leaving the physical beans we have come close to the metaphysical beans. Now, harvest the remaining beans, cultivate the wasteland, sow the beans, and turn the entire island into a bean patch. Then, feed on the beans, be stuffed with beans, and become wise bean pods! The clamor these words caused was as extreme as "beans fried in a clay pan," so to speak. The believers immediately surrounded our teacher, tore him apart, and hungrily ate him up. But after calming down "just as fried beans grow cold," they were astounded by the situation they themselves had brought about, and loudly cried in sorrow. In tears they rose to their feet, harvested the remaining beans, cultivated the wasteland, and sowed the beans. Now the whole island is a bean patch. Not so much a bean patch as a bean paradise. People feed on beans, are stuffed with them. Some even make a brazen pronouncement on our teacher that he was an imposter, who while banning the beans to us ate the beans himself — the proof is that when we put his flesh in our mouths it had an unmistakable taste of beans. But we say here: By the beans, we swear such was not the case. Furthermore, our teacher did not die. He has simply hidden himself from us; he is manifest in every bean. We believe in this, just as we believe in beans. Do not doubt this by any beans.

3

"Don't pick up a stone and strike that dog.
Do you not know it's your mother who ate beans?"
There are as many mothers as dogs in the world.
Mothers, on all fours, devour beans.
Their sons, in tears, are watching this.

"The essence of the world is number.
The number can be counted with beans."
The beans are dried and put on a wooden tray.
The barefoot students learn of the numbers in the tray.
The essence of the world that can be counted with beans is
        lonesome.

"The beans of the soul go through the circle of man,
the animal of the land, the animal of the sea, and the animal of
        the sky."
The green souls of the green beans,
the black-eyed souls of the black-eyed beans —
the beans eternally pass by one another in the sky.

"Turn your flesh into a pot for storing beans,
not into a clay pan for frying them."
You are a fragile, unglazed pot.
In it lies a single dried-up bean.
Outside the pot is always the evening of starvation.

THE DAY OF FIRE

1

Because it was the day of fire,
at every house, furniture and things that became unnecessary,
chairs, tables, cabinets, and beds were brought out
and burnt spiritedly in front of the door or near the gate.
All over the field called the field of vision, far and near,
innumerable columns of fire rose and rose,
pointing straight at heaven.

2

That day, I put together in one volume the poems
I had written for a long time for the one I loved,
knelt on the floor, and offered it to him in a reverential posture.
My loved one slapped it down on the floor the moment he
        received it.
Upon hitting the floor, the verses spouted fire and burnt up.
The face of my loved one, looking at me, burnt white with
        derision.
My face and my heart burnt black with shame.

3

That day, all the rivers were burning.
The domestic animals that went down to the river and drank,
        the cows and sheep,
burnt with fiercer thirst.
Gathering the burning rivers, the sea was burning in the
        distance.
In the burning sea were burning fish
and in the burning boats, burning fishermen,
who cast burning nets woven of burning yarn.

4

That day, I left the one I loved
and secluded myself in my room, facing my desk, the paper on
     my desk.
My fingers once again took up the pen for writing verses,
but what dripped from its tip was not ink
but the fire of fierce anger, its burning drips.
The drips of the fire of anger burnt the paper
in the shapes of the characters I wrote, no, in the shape of
     my anger.

5

I threw away the burning pen and, the burning door behind me,
began to walk as a traveler burning up, beginning with my hair.
On the membrane called the retina stands upside down
     gentle shower.
Rather, toward a single uncertain, cool drop of water
the trees, stones, dust, and all were burning,
because the day was the day of fire all over the earth,
because it was a small day of fire preparing for a great day
     of fire.

AN AMBIGUOUS PORTRAIT BASED ON QUOTATIONS FROM EIGHT PEOPLE

At 8:55 p.m., on May 7, while hurrying home from a meeting of the "Bridge Club," a small group who study the words and phrases of nō plays, I was crossing Meiji Street in Hara-juku, when a car hit me. I was carried by ambulance to the Kita-Aoyama Hospital, which was the closest hospital. The parts in quotation marks in the following poem are the remarks of the driver of the car, the ambulance medic on duty, a nurse, a friend who came to see me, a policeman on duty, a doctor who sewed me up, a surgeon specializing in brain nerves, and a magazine editor. I am entirely responsible for the arbitrariness in quotation, the willfulness in connecting quoted remarks to other sentences, and all the rest. Written on May 31.

"Are you all right?"
I am not all right.
Well then, are you done in?
I don't mean I'm done in.
Somewhere between all right and done in,
on a line of ambiguity the color of violet,
you are "seated."
"Don't walk."
Until when?
Probably until you begin to walk.

*

You are "contused" like a king,
all over your body, especially "your head and shoulders."
Your constant contusions are your *stigmata*,
even though you appear "not to be bleeding."

Therefore, you are "bandaged."
Since five thousand years ago, no, the eternal past,
you, bandaged, "hold on to the wall"
gray with time, "walk slowly,"
go up or down the stairs,
and return "to your bed," which is simple and ark-shaped.

*

"The bandages are" always "moving out of place."
From evening to morning you "lie still," asleep,
but during an eternity they move out of place,
one centimeter in a thousand years, five centimeters in five
      thousand years.
"We won't change your bandages."
Taking advantage of the itchiness from the bandages that moved
      out of place,
have the one "meal" in every five thousand years, for which you
      aren't too eager.
They "must quickly put away the tray."
"The unfinished meal is messy,"
especially when peered at through the lens of eternity.

*

You are "no longer young."
Also no longer "agile, either."
No, the restrictive phrase, *no longer*, isn't appropriate.
From the very moment you were born into this world
you were fully aged, and with feet of clay.
"Take this opportunity to have a long, restful sleep."
But you've been asleep all along.
The sureness of that sleep is almost diamond.
Running into that precisely polyhedral hardness,
"the other party" will be "shattered."

53

*

Does "a place you can't walk across"
exist for you?
In your state of sleep
you always "cross" time.
That's often where you turn left,
sometimes "a zebra-zone for turning right."
The zebras of time endlessly, soundlessly
are turning left, or turning right.
What you cross is not a road
but the herd of zebras that "came running to turn there."

*

"A hat for a thinking head,"
particularly for the head "like a rotten potato"
that crashed into the thought of time.
We must cover it with a kingly crown of stone to stop the
        sprouting,
the sprouting of sheer madness the color of cyanic acid.
It's vital "not to collect blood."
Because blood becomes a nutrient for the sprouting,
have all of it sent over there,
to the blessed head, which doesn't require a hat,
of "a laborer" the color of leather under the sun.

*.

"Let's try to slice" your "brain"
as if slicing with a slicer
the granite you lifted out of the darkness of the soil.
The previous evening, take the bandage off your globe of worry,
"Wash your hair well, but don't use shampoo."
All the "marks of collisions" since eternity,
the density of fog, even the blood clots the size of an adzuki bean,

"The film won't overlook anything."
A slice the color of ham of a community illusion called time,
your drifting brain is a pure metaphor for illusion.

      *

"For the author his work" is always an accident.
The fissure of time by the name of accident, its fissure lines.
You yourself are a drawing repeatedly redrawn
with a bunch of fissure lines of "quotations and allusions."
When the "bunch of quotations" is taken away
that structures your make-believe portrait,
naked king, who are you?
You, with your loosened face, your outline melted,
continue to walk, toward "the deadline is the end of the month"
the light at the end, or toward the darkness of resurrection.
Once again, "Are you all right?"

ON THE REALITY OF A POT

1

There is a pot.

2

The fact that there is a pot is not more certain than the certainty of the syntax that says there is a pot.

3

To make factually certain that there is a pot, the position of the pot, for example, on the axis of co-ordinates may be set. For now, the pot is in the darkness. Definitely outside the line of vision of my, or your, wide open eyes.

4

It is probably useful also to limit the darkness. For example, a corner of a kitchen made by piling up cut stones, the space below a dangling bunch of garlic, the tip of a whisker of a Chinese cricket, a line of light from the skylight — also outside any of these.

5

Next, we make limits within the limits and set its position in the darkness. Its ass on the oven built directly on the earthen floor (or rather by putting stones in the shape of !_!), it has a wooden lid on top. "On top" means simply "facing the ceiling," but because the sheer darkness there doesn't reveal the ceiling, the upper-lower relations carry no meaning. (Of course, the space below the bunch of garlic, too, is meaningless, and the tip of a whisker of the Chinese cricket also becomes meaningless.)

6

This means that to say the vigorous tongue of fire is licking the tail of the pot from below is also meaningless. If the expression, "from below," is meaningless, the expression, "tail of the pot," naturally becomes meaningless. Because the tail exists as something opposed to the head and, in an upright being, the two imply upper-lower relations.

7

As long as upper-lower relations do not make sense, you can't necessarily say of fire that it's licking the pot. The expression, "The pot is licking the fire," won't be wrong, either.

8

Here, let us digress somewhat and anecdotally consider the fire. That the fire is coming out of the wood placed on the earthen floor is no more than one possible explanation. If, for example, we are to take into consideration the match which was the direct cause of the fire in this instance, it will be more appropriate to explain that there is a certain amount of time between the wood, which, because of the fire that came from elsewhere, is in the transitional process from wood to carbon (and ultimately to ash), and the pot. Of course, you must at the same time think of reversing the order of "*wood* and *pot*" to "*pot* and *wood*."

9

Well, then, is it possible to say that the fire came from the match? It will be far more accurate to say that even with the match the fire came from elsewhere to it, no, to the space between the compound at the tip of the match-stick and the compound on the side of the match-box (match-stick and match-box may be reversed) and stayed at the tip of the match-stick for a certain amount of time.

10

If that is the case, where did the fire come from? Is it that in some invisible place there is the ideated world or hometown of fire and it has been called out to signal the friction between the tip of the match-stick and the side of the box? Or is it that one of the seeds of fire which are everywhere in the field of air has been made to sprout by a sudden stimulation? We will leave to the future the unknowability of this conjecture, as it is.

11

If we could make a transition from the uncertainty of the fire to the certainty of the pot, we certainly would be happy. No, it is fully possible that such happiness is no more than our wishful thinking.

12

At any rate, let's begin with the shape and the size of the pot. As for the shape, we will choose that of the traveler's hat of the ancient god of the road, the skull of the enemy commander which was also used as a wine cup at the victory banquet, the grave which the convict is forced to dig for himself, the mortar-shape of hell pictured in our imagination . . . in short, wide-mouthed, deep, and as conspicuously special-shaped as possible. As for the size, its diameter is about the length of the lower arm of an adult male. Its depth is approximately the length from the wrist to the elbow. But as something made by hand, the size is irregular. That is to say, both the diameter and the depth may differ slightly, depending on where you measure them.

13

If its shape and size are special, it is desirable that the material be also special. One would hope it is shoddy pig iron made by stepping on the foot-bellows and containing a good deal of impure elements. Therefore, it is on the whole thick and uneven. Because it has remained intimate with fire for at least a hundred fifty to sixty years in time (assuming there is time), the parts that are directly exposed to fire and the parts that aren't have changed differently: either thinning by heating or increasing in thickness through the attachment of soot. There are differences in parts, but on the whole it is as black as if the darkness around it had condensed. It may indeed be the condensed darkness, not "as if."

14

Let us continue for convenience. If, as we say conveniently, fire is burning outside, something is cooking inside. This is what's called logic. The most fragile fiction.

15

Something . . . like beans. Like oatmeal. Like overripe tomatoes. Like meat with bones. . . . It may simply be water. Even the air. Or vacuum. Though it must be vacuum as substance.

16

Why are we concerned that it must be some substance? Because if the reality of the pot remains uncertain after all this description, we will want to make the certainty of what's in it guarantee the certainty of the container.

17

Still, if what's cooking is vacuum, the pig iron that is the material of the pot itself will cook and diminish in weight though only little by little. But wait. The pig iron may not be diminishing, but merely moving elsewhere. That will be the case, especially if the pig iron is a metaphor for the condensed darkness.

18

The darkness is a container. Rather, the notion of container starts out from the darkness. If your brain is thinking about the true nature of what's cooking in that darkness, what's cooking may well be your brain. Will you say the brain, too, is no more than a metaphor for the darkness?

19

There is a pot, we began. It could have been a shoe, a jute bag, an armory, a measure for wheat, a silkworm moth, a horse-bean pod, or any other thing.

20

Even so, we chose a pot over everything else, because a pot is thought to be extremely common and boringly certain. But, for now, we must pay attention to the point, "is thought." When it comes to where the pot, which is thought to be certain, came from, we must say that our conjecture is cast in the unknowable darkness, just like our conjecture on where the fire, which is thought to be uncertain, came from.

21

That there is a pot is that there is darkness. This is the same as saying we are. That is, the darkness called us has conjectured the reality or the unreality of the darkness called a pot. Or, the reverse of that.

from
PRISM

WE, THE ZIPANGU PEOPLE

*Zipangu is the first Western name for Japan,
a spelling Marco Polo (1254-1324) gave to Ji-pun-guo,
the Chinese pronunciation of Nippon-koku.*

The island, draped in golden clouds,
does not exist anywhere on the chart.
We, the residents of the island, too,
do not exist anywhere in reality.
The sea of merchant Marco Polo's fantasy —
contiguous with it, the sailors'
cerebral ocean in whose storm we float, drift,
we, the so-called Zipangu people:
a multitude who are in the end an illusion, a dream,
     non-existent.
Never believe our word.

IF YOU ARE TO DISCUSS THE EYES

1

If you are to discuss the eyes, first,
you will in the end never learn about the eyes.
This is because for you eyes
mean no other than your eyes
and it is in the end demonstrably impossible
for your eyes to look at your eyes.

You gouge your eyes out with your right hand
and place them on the flat surface of the palm of your left hand.
When you do so, the holes from which the eyes have been
        removed
are not looking at the eyes on the palm,
but the twitching eyes are looking at
the two bloody, vacant holes.

Therefore, push your eyes on your palm
back into the darkness where they used to be.
Push into the darkness again the ambition
to look at your eyes with your own eyes,
and throw into the mud the formula that relates
the seer with the seen, in its frizzy state.

2

What we know about the dark box called *camera obscura* is
almost dark. As for its size, they say it is smaller than the atomic
nucleus caught in our speculative microscope, or that it is larger
than the expanding universe our imaginary telescope continues
to chase. As for its shape, it is said to be globular or cubic or, as
one theory holds, it is shapeless as a nebula or a sea slug. As for
its interior, the matter is even more uncertain, but as long as it's

called a dark box, it must have a peeping window of a specific size somewhere on its external circumference. This is because, without a peeping window, you cannot know whether or not the inside is dark. Therefore, the darkness of the inside must be that which corresponds to the volume of light that goes in through the peeping window, or the darkness that can be expressed by the semi-darkness before day-break or after sunset. What is it that is in that semi-darkness? The eye to determine that must become small or large in response to the size of the peeping window or, to put it differently, the size of the dark box; the logical conclusion suggests, however, that that which is caught by the eye peeping in has to be the eye peeping out. No, 'peeping out' is the willful speculation on the part of the eye peeping in; what is there is an eye seeing nothing, in fact the shapeless Only One, and this Only One, utterly unconcerned with The Other, has to be endlessly repeating its endless masturbatory act. That is the only reason for being of the dark box. If so, what is the reason for being of the dark box peeping into that dark box? Our speculations on the dark box go back to the twilight of all speculations.

3

"Replace correctly the three tenses
of 'see, saw, will see,' with the three tenses, no,
non-tenses, of 'don't see, didn't see, won't see,' "
you said with a quiet smile on your face.
"You will see that your forms of existence
of 'are, were, will be' are the three forms of existence, no,
correctly, forms of non-existence, of 'aren't, weren't, won't be.'"

I "see, saw, will see," no,
"don't see, didn't see, won't see" you going off
in the field called a field of vision.
You "are, were, will be," no,
"aren't, weren't, won't be" in front

beyond the uncertain line called a line of vision.
All this is an illusion that rises from the lake called Lake
    Lachrymal.

TWO EXCHANGES ON *L'OBJET D'ART*, SHOES

Make shoes, not poems — A German saying.

1

Lady, having accommodated your beautiful feet,
the shoes now trace your feet.
The palms of my hands holding up the shoes for your feet
trace the shoes and, therefore, your feet.
So, I, your faithful servant,
trace you, my haughty mistress.
I, a man, become a woman by tracing you,
and you, a woman, become a man by being traced.
I and you change places like night and day,
and man and woman change places like winter and spring.
Wearing the shoes and, therefore, your feet,
the palms of my hands are now beautiful feet.

2

Your Excellency, in accordance with the rules, you are dressed
    correctly,
put your ass correctly on the seat, face the table correctly.
On the dustless white table-cloth, a highly polished large
    white plate.
I, in servant's guise, arrive and, from a large tin pot held to
    one side,
place on the plate not meat, not fish, but a black
    high-heeled shoe.
You take the silver knife and fork, set them down where
    they were,
and lift them yourself with such impeccable elegance.
Again following the rule, you hesitate somewhat before licking
    lightly, first,

·

the decorative leather at the heel, next the toe leather, to which
     you then apply your strong teeth.
About an hour later now, you have your jacket removed, tie
     loosened,
socks taken off, and even pants and underwear lowered,
your forehead drenched in sweat, more than half of the shoe
     already in your mouth.
But when I slowly turn my point of view from you to the shoe,
more than half of your face, beginning with the mouth, is
     swallowed by the shoe.
I ought to rush to you in consternation, but what can I do:
Having already changed my guise from servant to shoe,
I have swallowed you, you who have metamorphosed your
     entire self into a foot, beginning with your head.

TABLE MANNERS

A formally dressed, well-mannered, young gentleman,
you must make the lady to your right feel relaxed.
But she won't even be able to look at you, eye to eye,
because what those two crossed hands hold are not
a knife and fork, but a sickle and halberd.
(You can tell without turning to look)
Like a shy boy you will stare at your hands.

                    *

You shall not tuck your napkin into your pants or belt.
More intolerable is to tie it around your neck.
But the well-starched white cloth will not escape the destiny
        of affixation
because your knees shake uncontrollably, without interruption,
and seem unable to hold anything on them.
(Perhaps it is your neck that wants to be affixed?)
If we are to name your ailment, it may well be *napkin complex*.

                    *

You shall not jump to the plate served like a starved wild dog.
You shall not forget that you belong to the proud order of
        Primates.
But the plate will not be able to avoid a bestial, crude assault
because if you eat elegantly, appropriate to your bow-tie,
you can't help seeing the horrible reality of what you're eating.
(With a gentleman, excessive vulgarity is often a proof of
        conscience)
Your plate that continues to clink and clatter will be the object to
        be frowned at by all those present.

*

You shall stab the meat with your fork, cut it with your knife,
and carry one slice at a time to your mouth.
But this agreement can't but be ignored at times
because if you're engaged in an open and fair act,
you shouldn't need ritualistic excuses.
(You begin to see a wild dog's decorum at the meal)
You will again take up your fork and knife.

*

Let us keep in mind: it is embarrassing to pour the wine
into your mouth, fork held in your left hand.
But in the end the glass, like the fork, will be on one side of
        the scale
because what you're eating is your brother,
the blood-dripping flesh of your loved one you murdered.
(To forget the blood that was shed, this blood-colored liquid!)
You must keep your remorse and drunkenness as close to each
        other as you can.

*

The finger bowl is a metal tub for the fingers.
It isn't a pool for both hands to bathe in.
But the water won't *not* overflow the brim of the bowl
because the lady to your right, who has paled,
you can tell, is deliberately washing her raw-smelling hands in it.
(You also know her teeth are smeared with blood)
You take off your napkin and wipe your hands in great haste.

70

*

When the dinner's over, you place your knife and fork where
    they were.
You shall not rise to your feet before those in senior stations do.
But you cannot rise to your feet before or after
because what has vanished from your plate is not your brother,
but, in fact, your self devoured by your loved one.
(The essence of manners is to make yourself void in
    following them)
The lady to your right has also vanished unbeknownst to you.

BLIND DAY

In Karuizawa, on July 31, 1981: the opening of a
Marcel Duchamp show at the Takanawa Museum

With a shard of glass that the black tip of the tongue of a candle
      was made to lick, we did not peep at the blind sun.
Because fine raindrops filled the space from the iris to the sun
we talked about a fleet steed born in a blindfolded stable in the
      darkness of day.
Was not the mother of this excellent specimen famous in the
      annals of horses blind?
The blindness of whiskey was licking the coasts of the glasses in
      our hands.
We did our best trying to ignore the "painter," the excuse for our
      having been invited.
But how many were those gathered at the party surrounding his
      widow that night.
A widow is always the mother of her husband who died. Her
      white hair, her smile, and her vigorous appetite, too.
Throngs of rain with white shins were laying siege to the
      golf-house in the field.
Breaking through the armies of rain, the guests dashed one after
      another.
The guests were only brides and bachelors, bachelors and
      brides, and bachelors.
Of course, this included virgin brides and wedded bachelors.
Thinking that they were casually moving about from drinks to
      food to gossip,
the guests were certainly being manipulated by the will of
      someone.
If God already doesn't exist, who was the one manipulating
      them?
Was it not that an extraordinarily talented monsieur who

dreamed of becoming an ordinary monsieur,
no, a moustachioed mademoiselle by the name of Rose,
was stretching her delicate fingers out of the raincloud, the
    mother of the lances of rain,
and moving us as chessmen?
But a peep-hole through which to peep at this mother's son as
    well as her lover
is not prepared for us. Or, when we peep
what is on the other side of the peep-hole is already a corpse.

FOLLOWING THE KEY WORDS

Panihida to Daniel Shigeo Washisu

Daniel Shigeo Washisu was born, in 1915, of a poor family
who were Russian Orthodox and formerly of the samurai
class. During the great earthquake of 1923, he lost his mother
and his youngest brother. During World War II he fought in
various parts of China. After Japan's defeat, he tried to settle
as a farmer in Hokkaido, Japan's northernmost island, but
couldn't manage it and ended up changing his job fifteen or
sixteen times. He spent his last ten years in Saitama as a writer
and a poet. Though afflicted with a great many chronic
illnesses, he mastered more than ten languages, ancient and
modern, on his own, and wrote lyrical and religious poetry
with strong themes. He also wrote about poetry and religion.
His position in modern Japanese poetry is without compare.
He died in 1982.

1

"Mother is in me.
In me, my young mother is
hugging tight my young father, of the past,
at the apex of her bliss,"
you mutter, a white-haired boy-peeper into what's between
    the thighs.
Beyond, a scorched-smelling copy of the end of the world
    standing on its hands.
The eternal mother-god is eternally beautiful
as she supports heaven's beam spouting fire with her white
    shoulders
to protect the Holy Spirit who is her husband and son.
The infant boy who sucks her nipple full of blood

before long turns into a bearded infant — the young mother
     in him,
in the young mother, the young powerful father.
You, who are mythically endowed with both sexes,
begin to stride across the heavenly dome which is the corpse of
     the goddess;
you put on army boots, take up a bayonet, march,
and kill countless young fathers and young mothers.
Your head crowned with ash, you beat your breast so hard that
     the ribs almost break,
and, dripping uncontrollable blood your crotch bent forward,
plant dying sweet potatoes on a mist-cold mountain top.
"Because in the dark ecstacy of the embrace it brings,
by force, an unrelated, innocent soul from the other world,
procreation is a deeply rooted sin,"
you mutter sadly, now older than your father and mother,
and suddenly fall silent.

2

"The dead equally encircle death
and keep the door of death closed, which no force
seems able to open,"
you once said.
You always, always talked about death,
about the dead, about the appeasement of the dead.
You sometimes talked about the living, but only as the
     reflections of the dead.
After talking about the dead, you became a dead one,
after talking about death, you belonged to death.
By your death, by your metamorphosis to a dead one,
the dead's encirclement of death relaxed for a moment,
and the door of death was opened slightly for us.
"You don't say you die,
you say you fall asleep,"
you also said.

3

"I eat father, eat mother,
eat people, eat God, and soon
I will deliver myself again
to the Other."
These are the words you've left.
I am the Other you meant, and my greedy hands,
to which you delivered yourself, lie on the table.
My fingers are sticky with sweet rice, which is you,
my tongue is wet with water, which is you.
As soon as your teeth ceased mastication of the Other,
the wandering of your blood and flesh began.
You were baked in the oven and, ground
and sown, became ash, became soil,
became wheat, became grapes, became seeds of grapes.
At the end of the intestinal labyrinths of fowl and fish,
dreaming of blinding floods of light,
you continue the long journey of silence.
I will happily be bored by you.
"In the most physical guise
love exists as food."
These too are your bright words.

AH, OH

Once, on some occasion, I said to Shigeo Washisu, "If the Ah's
and Oh's disappeared from your writings, they'd feel so much
more clean." Here's what he said in reply: "Ah, you're right.
Oh, that's true, you're right." Two years since he descended
into the Underworld and, stripped of his temporary
personality known as Shigeo Washisu, became death in
general, I wanted to call to him using Ah's and Oh's
abundantly. Ah, Oh, true enough, I wanted to call to him.

Ah, this land is sick.
 Oh, is the soil there fertile?
Ah, what thrives here are stones and weeds.
 Oh, do a lot of heads with disjointed neck bones fructify?
Ah, both poetry and potatoes are skinny and dry.
 Oh, are the words exploding like the nuts of the dead?
 (Ah, Oh, the nuts of the dead, shattered brainpans, also
  called scrotums)
Ah, the underground river escapes the vertically shaking
 earth's crust.
 Oh, does the thick river haze of oblivion cover the ground?
Ah, I dig and dig, but only yellowed white hair.
 Oh, is the pubic hair of the soil glistening wet?
Ah, I seek and seek, but only despair turned brownish white.
 Oh, is even despair refreshing again and again?
 (Ah, Oh, there, even despair revives again and again.)
Ah, the handle of a hoe can only become dry and break
 into two.
 Oh, is the steel amply soaked in the night air?
Ah, the nails can only become deformed and crack into
 numberless fissures.
 Oh, do the nails and whiskers continue to grow night
  and day?

Ah, the eyes and the breasts become wrinkled and irritatingly
     pointed.
          Oh, are the breezes through the trees black and delicate?
          (Ah, Oh, the trees of the Underworld are equipped with
               eyes and breasts.)
Ah, the starved baby weeps, impatient with the nipples that
     only give blood.
          Oh, is even your old, smelly mouth bored with milk?
Ah, under the man's excitement, the woman is the fire that
     burns midsummer thorns.
          Oh, is lust properly kept cooled?
Ah, here the fire, too, is frazzled.
          Oh, are the flames velvety and pliant?
          (Ah, Oh, our fire is a clumsy copy of the fire of the
               Underworld.)
Ah, it merely scorches uselessly and doesn't purify anything.
          Oh, do burnt things learn of the peace of the ash?
Ah, the dog that swallowed the sun thrashes about on the
     horizon.
          Oh, does the eternal twilight change the barking dog into a
               gentle shadow?
Ah, I look up at the uphill path and, with my brow knit,
     continue to ask.
          Oh, he continues to descend on the other side of the path,
               wiping off his sweat.
          (Ah, Oh, his ears will never hear my voice.
          That can never happen. Ah, Oh.)

EPITAPH FOR THE POET HIMSELF

Ancient Japanese poetry has *makura-kotoba*, pillow words,
which correspond to epithets in ancient Greek poetry. Here,
shiranu hi, in the Chinese characters, means "unknown fire"
and modifies Tsukushi (present-day Fukuoka and, more
broadly, the Island of Kyushu).

The land of fine pedigree with the pillow-word
"unknown fire" gave birth to me.
I realized the deep significance this fact had,
God forbid, only when I thirsted for the last drop of water.
The very culprit who drove me to countless loves
and one poem, on a pilgrimage that gave no time
to tying shoe-strings and untying them
was, who else, this dark unknown flame.
The same furious fire goes on, unabated,
an allows the bones under the mound to rest, at no time.

DECLARATION OF LOVE FOR DOLLS

1

Where does our love for dolls come from,
Pygmalion?
The yellow father with an umbrella pushes a cart in an alley
and the pallid mother treadling at her sewing machine is raped
    at the entrance door.
The one who rapes her is not a personality
but a hirsute, sweaty establishment in a surgeon's smock.
I feel the dark bulk of its back in the next room.
I hate the weak-willed father, I hate the unresisting mother,
I hate the emotionless coitus between father and mother that
    brought us forth.
We look down, curl up
and can't but simulate a parturition on the *tatami* floor.
In the distance a voice, a waste-paper dealer, passes.
It's the slow morning of a spring day
when the odor from the toilet permeates the main street.

2

As for our sex, we are neither male nor female
much less neuter.
A boy: neither the third nor the fourth, always the sex of
    number zero.
So, like euglenas or common jellyfish
we endlessly carry out our transparent monogenesis.
The copies of us that go on multiplying endlessly
fill up the small room, spill down through the spaces between
    the *tatami* floor,
go outside through the cracks of the windowpanes, and are
    blown in the wind.
If a term "imagined pregnancy" exists,

a term "imagined delivery" might as well exist.
Imagination is a form of existence.
This is true.
Pygmalion,
like a pregnant woman who has given too many childbirths, we
     have grown old while young
and with a black eye, convulse ceaselessly.

3

The doll: it's a concept before it is a thing,
an idea packed more firmly with substance than a thing.
Because this substance is more delicate than cells or particles
it comes through the wall or papered-door and stands before us.
It dives in through our scalp and crouches in our brain.
Our skull comes to resemble a uterus more and more.
To deliver a doll, to give birth to it through the two irises and
     the tips of the ten fingers —
Pygmalion,
it doesn't have the kind of entrails or soul that we have in us.
No, instead of entrails or a soul, their absence fills it.
The shining surface of its body covering a substance called
     absence is not even material.
Is it a he? Or a she? If our sex is that of a boy,
its sex is that of a doll. If we are number zero, it's the nth sex.

4

The knife, the saw, the pliers, the hammer, the file,
the pincers, the scissors, the vice, the drill, the calipers,
rubber tape, rubber gloves, cotton, the drier . . . .
how these implements to make dolls
resemble the implements to kill a man!
Pygmalion,
we do not make dolls to resemble us,
we make ourselves resemble dolls the best we can.
May father be remade, may mother be remade,

may the deformed flesh coming out of father and mother be
    remade.
If they can no longer be remade, let them be annihilated.
The head and the torso, legs and arms, eyeballs and tongue, hair
    and pubic hair —
to dissect is to link or, to put it differently,
to kill is to give birth.

5

Is it possible to bring death to a doll?
This is the ultimate subject of our love for the doll.
How are we to determine medically the time of death
of a doll that has no brain or heart?
The head pulled off from the body,
the eyeballs gouged out of the eye-sockets,
are staring at our hands without expression.
Even if we swing down our hammer on them,
smash them, and break them apart,
the afterimage of the eyeballs will continue to stare.
Not only the head, not only the eyeballs,
the navel, the crotch, the palms, the soles,
every part is staring at us.
If it was live even before birth,
how is it possible to kill it?
Pygmalion,
we are dead before being killed.

from
THE GARDEN OF RABBITS

THE GARDEN

You talked about an imagined garden
where a real toad lived.
but now that you, who talked about it, has left,
what is the garden, what is the toad?
The garden was you, and the toad was
your brain that crouched in your center.
The brain turned to dust, keeping its shape,
was little by little carried away by the wind,
and is now all gone, leaving no trace. So now
the toad lives only in the words you've left
or in their memory, and the garden exists
only with that shadowy toad.
When we secretly revive those words
with our trembling tongues, in the rain,
we become a rainy garden, our brain
a wet toad licking the rain,
and slowly begin to walk. Apart from that toad,
there is no garden called us.

A STUDY OF WEEDS

"In the world of weedy plants
there is constant competition for survival.
There appear to be some plants
that exude substances that are harmful
to other plants."
When you, in junior high school, said this
in your report printed on cheap mimeographed paper,
you knew nothing about the souls of the plants;
you did not know about the soulful substances
that the souls of the plants exuded from their soulful bodies.

   "It was not me.
   It was my soul who killed my brother.
   Therefore, please punish not me
   but my soul. I committed
   no crime."
   So pleaded a criminal.
   If he's saying the soul of a man
   exists slightly outside the man as an actual image,

   the soul of the American golden rod
   exists slightly outside the American golden rod.
   The act of the soul of the American golden rod,
   however, cannot but give a definite influence
   to the American golden rod itself.
   The act of the soul of the man who killed his brother
   forces the man himself to stand on the gallows.

You pushed aside the growth of American golden rod
slightly outside the soul of the American golden rod, swaying,
and went out into the human world —
you certainly had a soul slightly outside yourself, swaying.

Was it you or was it your soul
who said the following in the same report:
"Where last year American golden rod
was conspicuous, its number is
a great deal less this year. Its substance
that is harmful to other plants
may be destructive to itself at the same time."

ANTI-ANGELICO

Even Hell is always stolen.
At the same time there is no Maria genuflecting in the
     colonnade,
there exists no Eva being driven out of the garden.
It's a long time since the two angels, of goodness and evil,
were both erased from the painting.
"A seductive prostitute, a savior saint —
neither role is my cup of tea."
Yes, you're right, my eternal, terrifying companion.
To be sure, the good woman and the bad
are both pitiable illusions of pitiable men.
That we've been robbed of Heaven doesn't mean
we have in its stead Hell where we can live in peace.
Time which is no time, a place which is no place —
there I must till the frozen ground with you, lady,
no matter how unfamiliar that sound may be to my ear,
I must know your true name.

MONKEY-EATERS

I'd like to paint monkey-eaters,
like the painter who painted potato-eaters.
(Outside there's blizzard, inside fire's burning)
There's no difference between them: eating potatoes
under a lamp, and eating monkeys in a forest.
Just as when you eat potatoes the blood of potato courses
       through your blood vessels,
when you eat monkeys the blood of monkeys courses through
       your blood vessels.
Just as potato-eaters become potatoes,
monkey-eaters become monkeys. If the blood of the monkeys
is filled with death, they become monkeys of death.
(Death is burning red, life becomes invisible in the blizzard)
A monkey-eater who becomes a monkey of death isn't someone
who has nothing to do with me. Someone who devours a
       monkey of death, beginning with its head,
who becomes a monkey of death and screams, is me, no
       one else.
(The blood of the monkey of death who's tearing itself apart
       with sorrow
is fiercely dreaming of making my blood the blood of the
       monkey of death)
Now I've taken up my brush, in the manner of the painter
who painted himself eating potatoes and becoming a potato
and became a potato, beginning with his fingers holding
       the brush.
(Life is a blizzard, it's blizzard, it's burning)

ECHO

I am a hornbill.
I am a chameleon.
I am a gazelle.
I am a wart hog, a large-eared elephant, a hippopotamus.
I am someone who is a hornbill, a chameleon, a gazelle, a wart
      hog, a large-eared elephant, a hippopotamus.
I am you.
You must know you are someone who is a hornbill, a
      chameleon, a gazelle, a wart hog, a large-eared elephant,
      a hippopotamus.
You are me.
I who am you and you who are me are one person.
That one person is carved into a mask and painted as someone
      who is a hornbill, a chameleon, a gazelle, a wart hog, a
      large-eared elephant, a hippopotamus.
That mask is me, that mask is you.
The mask that is me and the mask that is you are one person.
I do not exist apart from the mask, you do not exist apart from
      the mask, I who am you and you who are me do not exist
      without the mask.
He is someone who was and is.

THE BAD RABBIT

1

The rabbit is a bad animal.
When castaways released some to the island,
they ate grass and mated, they mated and proliferated,
and ate up all the grass there was on the island.
The castaways starved to death, and the rabbits, too, died out.
The earlier settlers, the small ducks, ran out of grass to eat,
so chased the innumerable flies that grow on the beach to keep
 themselves alive.
The island was covered with green grass again,
but the small ducks continue to chase gusts of flies.
Those who eat the grass are only the souls of the rabbits.
These long-eared souls eat and mate
and give birth to young long-eared souls one after another
on the island where for one hundred years the waves have come
 and gone with the same monotony.

2

Grandmother was born in the Year of the Rabbit
and was destined to be rabbity, mother says.
She made husbands of a number of men, who all passed away
 before she did,
and gave birth to a number of children, who died one after
 another.
Unsatiated, with the surviving kid on her back,
she let a neighborhood man violate her from behind in the
 woodshed
like the rabbits behind the wire net of the rabbit shed.
The kid on her back knew it, mother says,
because the kid was mother in her infancy.
Mother was born not in the Year of the Rabbit whose ears are

red inside,
but in the Year of the Ox crowned with two clumsy horns.
Grandmother is not to blame, mother says,
the rabbit that was stamped into her destiny is.
The rabbit comes around exactly every twelfth year
and is stamped into an inseminated destiny, rabbit-shape.

3

A roasted rabbit is delicious. It is especially delicious
when you hold it with both hands and bite into it.
A rabbit with well-developed front teeth and hind legs
looks less like an old hag than a boy, I think.
In reality the souls of long-eared rabbits
get into boys, get into old hags, that's all.
The soulless rabbit I'm eating
may no longer be a rabbit.
The soul of the sharp-toothed rabbit must be inside me,
eating the fake rabbit the boy's soul has gotten into,
holding it with both hands.
Behind me, eating, is always a picture
of the beautiful island with the souls of the rabbits.

ON THE BEACH

E. Pound's Grave

Rather than about your grave where laurel trees are planted
on this isle of graves enclosed by a high stone wall,
I'd like to talk about the flow coursing around this isle of graves,
    about the flow of time
moving beyond the fig trees, elderberries, and sorrels.
You are someone who came from the other shore to this,
someone who, even when alive, could not help thinking
about another shore while standing on one.
We cannot choose the other shore over this
but can only think about another from one.
We come to a shore, drifting.

A SKETCH FOR "TRAVELING MAN"

1

Traveling man, you are
the rush hat you wear deep down to your eyes.
Occupied by the territory of the shadow of its wide brim,
your expression can hardly be seen.
No, it can't be seen, not because of the hat,
but because of the handkerchief that covers your face.
No, no, even if the square of the handkerchief is removed,
what is there are the vacantly open mouth and nostrils.
Even the two eyes are now two vacant holes.
In reality you are what has leaked out
all at once from all those holes,
toward where the leaves scatter, the sun rotates noisily.

2

You are exactly like what you yourself had been
until just moments ago, the man parallel to the ground.
In your hand, a stick made of goosefoot stripped of its bark,
from your neck, a pilgrim's scrip of knit akebia fiber,
in the scrip, five bone-dry mottled kidney beans,
four wings of a spotted beetle ready to fall,
and eight black sharp claws of a squirrel monkey.
With these you can go anywhere:
the plain where grasses taller than you sway,
unimaginably deep waters on the other shore,
sky painful to the eyes above the top of a large tree,
and even the bottomless azure hole in the middle of the sky.

3

You are the smell of the water in which boiled rice was washed.

Because, before you left for these travels, your family
washed you clean, using a single-spout bowl,
neither your beard nor nails will grow while you travel.
Because your family, weeping, carefully cut them,
dug the ground, and threw them into it along with your clothes,
you will not remember while you travel
the beard and the nails, which were once yours,
even if the beard and the nails remember you.
A man who travels, without turning to look, leaving
a smell of porridge on the surface of the landscape, that's you.
In your mouth, dried rice and dried shellfish.

4

Your family carve wood
and make a table for you;
knead clay, turn the potter's-wheel, and bake flagons.
There are two flagons, for muddy liquor and clear liquor.
On the table, dried meat, salted meat, corn, millet,
green chestnuts, unpeeled, still left in their burrs;
bitter lettuce and fern being chewed
to remember you, the one missing
from the relaxed group surrounding the fire.
But the tears fragrant of hollyhock and violet
will not reach your nasal membrane:
your nose is stuffed with cotton flowers.

5

You're always, always thirsty,
thirsty not only for water, but thirsty for salt.
You wander, looking for water, looking for salt.
But this is an age lacking in water, salt destroyed. Where best
for you to seek them, under which rabble?
You catch a boy passing by and push him into a shadow,
lick the salt educed on his suntanned legs,
drink the green-smelling water from his green-smelling erection.

But when you grab his thighs and look up at him,
the boy, behind his convulsing neck, is as old as the world.
Vomiting violently, you continue to wander,
as one much thirstier than before.

6

You have no shadow in the first place,
yourself being a shadow,
but at times that shadow seems ready to fade.
You crouch under a tree, on the grasses.
They are a fragrant tree and wise grasses.
In the season that has withered away as far as you can see,
the fragrance ducks in through the cotton flowers stuffing
     your nose,
so there is no mistaking the fact that it is full of wisdom.
You inhale the fragrance of the clever plants to the full,
and, recovering your darkness somewhat, begin to walk again.
Blind winds and color-blind dogs are your close friends.
As you begin to walk, they trot in front, in back.

7

Fire, too, is your close friend, is he not?
He has no eyes, has no ears; he has no nose or mouth.
Rather, his whole being is an eye, an ear, a nose, a mouth.
His whole being is a hand and a leg.
He held to his bosom the one who was once you,
licked with his tongue the one who was once you.
Because that one already was no longer you,
you cannot possibly remember the fire at that time.
Besides, you are a man who travels without turning to look.
But when you see fire, you walk up close to it despite yourself.
Seeing you, the fire cries out joyfully,
at the height of his joy, how he sobs and weeps!

8

The road always spreads like a casting net before you.
As for the size of the net, it can more than cover the world.
No matter which road you take from any mesh of the net,
even if you walk past the world and go out into the sky or go
    underground,
the road never ends, your travels never end.
You pass the village and the town of the sky, walk through the
    underground forest.
At times you get on a boat and manipulate its oars with
    your wrists.
There, it's a wilderness called the sea, or a sea called the
    wilderness.
At times, you travel the life road of those who love you,
those who loved you so much they choked on your bones
    and ash,
a road which is a blood vessel, a seminal duct, a tear duct.
One morning, when you turn the faucet, you may spout out.

9

By the roadside, a house;
in the house a lamp is lit, under the lamp, merry noise.
Soon the gayeous noise ceases, the lamp goes out.
At the bottom of the darkness, hot whispers; then,
    suppressed moans.
Your ears stuffed with cotton flowers, pricked up
in the wind, are they listening, or are they not?
Outside the wall, you grow lighter, lighter, lighter.
How can you say that the two, devouring pleasure,
in their dark joy, will not pull you in from outside?
How can you say that when ten months and ten days
    have passed
you will not cry your birth-cry on the morning sheets in
    that house?
You that morning are a baby far older than the world.

RHETORICA

For the non-being that was (was not) Yukio Mishima

Fujiwara no Teika (1162-1241):
*As I look out, there are neither blossoms nor crimson
leaves: by a cove, a thatched hut, this autumn evening*

As   I   looked   out
there   were   no   blossoms   or
    crimson   leaves:
the   magic   by   so   saying   of
    conjuring   in   blank   space
blossoms   and   crimson   leaves   brilliantly,
the   trick   by   denying   that   they
    were   there
of   giving   them   sure   and   solid
    footing   isn't   it?
Your   lopped   head   pale   as
    blossoms   raw-smelling   as   crimson
    leaves
may   not   have   existed   from   the
    outset:
by   making   us   think   so   it
    has   occupied   a   blank   space
    with   assuredness.
This   was   your   rhetoric   of   blood-
    bathed   curse.
We   are   forced
to   turn   into   mere   noses   into
    mere   sniffing   functions
and   to   continue   eternally   to   sniff
    not   the   smell   of   your   blood
    not   your   actual   being
but   their   memory   more   certain
    than   they.
OE!

THREE POEMS

THE INVISIBLE BOOK

a Santiago

1

There is no one who has seen the book.
Yet there is no one who doubts its existence.
It sleeps in the depths of the distant clouds dark before dawn.
To awaken it from its sleep, which has neither form nor size,
our imagination is too poor, too weak.
What is now spread out in our lamp
is a metaphor, too neglible,
of that unimaginable book to come.

2

Let's try to see how effective a metaphor can be:
The number of pages of the book is much greater than
all the pages of all the books in the world added together.
The gilded top and bottom rims are farther apart than heaven
       and earth in the evening glow.
Its front cover and back cover are separated from each other,
farther than the horizon of the east from the horizon of the west.
The number of characters in this book . . . but this book
can neither be written in characters nor counted by page.

3

There is nothing that is not inscribed in this book.
All the pulses of the universe are inscribed.
Every vertical wrinkle of that rose is recorded.
The action in each second of every one of us — for example,
even each of the words I write down here,
or if I draw a line and erase my own description,

even that erasure is written in, leaving out nothing.
This description, too, is written in. So is *this* description.

4

Who are we in front of this book?
If we are not allowed to read it, but on the contrary
we are read closely by it,
is the book a mirror-like eye, and are we
the spilled types transfixed by the eye?
Is the book a heavily guarded savage jail, and are we
the prisoners chained in the dark of its cells, half dead?
Is it in the end impossible to reach the blue sky engraved in the
      iron bars?

5

Let us burn this ominous book while there is time,
before it shows itself in front of us.
If this is impossible, let us feed the tongues of burning fire
with these words strung together to chronicle it.
But if the incineration of the words, even the combustion of
      the book
is inscribed without exception, what will become of us?
The only way left is to throw ourselves into the flames of paper,
for ourselves to burn, to be recorded in the book of flames.

A TALE OF THREE CITIES

MILANO

To Kazuhiko Kumai

The priestess of Cumae, of Petronio,
dangling in the vacant space of a krater,
replied, "I'd like to die,"
but the sculptor Kumai, in 1986,
seems to tie krater-shaped eternal darkness
to a fleeting band of light, while actually untying it,
and while seeming to untie it, makes a puzzling ring by tying
    it again.
Shall we die, or shall we live?
Ducking in through the ring, or cutting it aside,
a traveler carrying a drawn length of steel: you.
Wrapped things: let them be opened. Or:
Opened things: let them be wrapped. These are
the beautiful magic words of the Mediolanum summer,
the sharp songs of the swallows crisscrossing the evening sky.

VENEZIA

To Alex Susana

This Alexander does not sigh by the Ganges
but enjoys taking walks along the canals of Venezia;
delights not in skillfully riding the stallion of Time to
    create history,
but in walking along the accessories of history;
wanders, an umbrella his stick, in the labyrinth of coincidences
    and inevitabilities, of water and stone,
at times wandering into a forgotten courtyard in a drizzle.
In the courtyard: a bush with no exit; on a wet trunk: the whorl

103

of a snail;
at the end of the labyrinth of existence: a wet, abandoned house,
    framed in whose window
are the lagoon of death and the island of death in twilight.
His high window facing the water remains lit throughout
    the night,
and the tip of his pen keeps spewing blue uncertain water.
But that feeble flow from a corner of his room
falls below through the gutter and fills the canals and the sea
    of death
with the island of death floating in it — this is also true.

FIRENZE

To Kimio Kawaguchi

Kimiko fell down the staircase, directly to hell,
Kimio up the staircase to the Renaissance paradise.
But can his pitiful soul bear the terror of renascence?
The rooms upstairs are closed in golden clouds.
Rather than grope the nine heavens in tempera,
go out to the plaza and leave your ass to a chair under
    the sun.
The red wine of Tuscia is bright, the white refreshing.
This is a lesson not only to the healthy body but to the soul.
The act of copying is, after all, no more than copying of an act.
Break your pencil in two and throw it into the muddy flow from
    the bridge.
The flow pours on to the sea, the sea never reaches
the shore of your hometown but the terrible precipice at the end
    of the world.
Straight down the precipice the water falls and, fortunately,
below it, there is no landscape you can paint.

LESSONS OF THE SAND

Despairing of the darkness gentle with human smells,
the two legs that have strayed out into the maze of light
are now on the sea of sand set afire by the sun right above.
Flaring up from the feet is a single voice of terrifying silence
congested with a hundred voices, and its congested echoes
are poured into two earholes:
"In a shadowless place all's clear" "All's clear"
"For a human everyone's always an enemy" "Always
        an enemy"
"All enemies must be destroyed" "Must be destroyed"
"Otherwise you'll be destroyed" "You'll be destroyed"
"The destroyer and the destroyed are brothers" "Are brothers"
"No one can come between the two" "Between the two"
"Blood that's shed is proof of its own innocence" "Its own
        innocence"
"Blood is soft and then is solid" "Then is solid"
The one who hears the clamor of silence that breaks in
through his covering fingers becomes black and deaf
and totters to the white village beyond the sand.
Those who have come out of the darkness of houses into
        the light,
stone held in each hand, corner him.
Sinking in the blood he himself spurts out,
his scream is as porous as the scream of the drowned.
"Love" boils up white, while lying black and cold.

BOOKS BY HIROAKI SATO

History and criticism:
One Hundred Frogs: From Renga to Haiku to English

Translations:
Poetry
Poems of Princess Shikishi
Ten Japanese Poets
Spring & Asura: Poems of Kenji Miyazawa
Mutsuo Takahashi: Poems of a Penisist
Lilac Garden: Poems of Minoru Yoshioka
Howling at the Moon: Poems of Hagiwara Sakutarō
See You Soon: Poems of Taeko Tomioka
Chieko and Other Poems of Takamura Kōtarō
A Bunch of Keys: Selected Poems by Mutsuo Takahashi
From the Country of Eight Islands: An Anthology of
    Japanese Poetry, with Burton Watson
A Future of Ice: Poems and Stories of a Japanese Buddhist,
    Miyazawa Kenji
Osiris, The God of Stone: Poems of Gōzō Yoshimasu

(In Japanese)
Nami Hitotsu (Translation of John Ashbery's book of poems, A
    Wave).

Prose
The Sword and the Mind

(In Japanese)
Eigo Haiku: Aru Shikei no Hirogari

Poems (in English)
That First Time: Renga on Love & Other Poems

Essays
Manhattan Culture School (English & Japanese)
Manhattan Bungaku Mampo (Japanese)

Printed in the USA
CPSIA information can be obtained
at www.ICGtesting.com
JSHW082221140824
68134JS00015B/664